DICKINSON PUBLIC LIBRARY

WID

3 4050 00098 9884

D0792280

Dickinson Public Library
44__ H__hw__ 3
Dickins__, T__ 77539__
281-534-3812

WID

12/12

Galveston County Library
System
Galveston Co.. Texas

DEMCO

PROP TRICKS

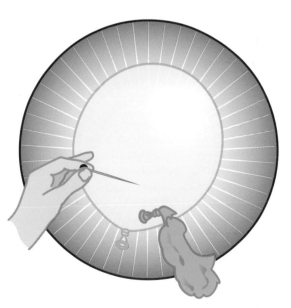

STEPHANIE TURNBULL

A⁺

Smart Apple Media

Galveston County Library
System
Galveston Co., Texas

Published by Smart Apple Media
P.O. Box 3263
Mankato, MN 56002

U.S. publication copyright © 2012 Smart Apple Media. International copyright reserved in all countries. No part of this book may be reproduced in any form without written permission from the publisher.

Printed in the United States of America at Corporate Graphics, in North Mankato, Minnesota.

Library of Congress Cataloging-in-Publication Data
Turnbull, Stephanie.
 Prop tricks / by Stephanie Turnbull.
    p. cm. -- (Secrets of magic)
 Includes index.
  ISBN 978-1-59920-499-4 (library binding)
 1. Magic tricks--Juvenile literature. 2. Stage props--Juvenile literature. I. Title.
 GV1548.T87 2012
 793.8--dc22

                                                2010045571

Created by Appleseed Editions, Ltd.
Designed and illustrated by Guy Callaby
Edited by Mary-Jane Wilkins
Picture research by Su Alexander

Picture credits
l = left, r = right, t = top, b = bottom
Contents page l Eline Spek/Shutterstock, r Ljupco Smokovski/Shutterstock; 4 Art Directors & Trip/Alamy; 5t Vladimir Mucibabic/Shutterstock, b Iconotec/Alamy; 8 Steve Bielschowsky/Alamy; 10 Zhu Difeng/Shutterstock; 12 Danylchenko Laroslav/Shutterstock; 14 & 15 Blueking/Shutterstock; 16 Robert Adrian Hillman/Shutterstock; 17 Hulton-Deutsch Collection/Corbis; 18 KBL Photo/Shutterstock; 20 Artur Synenko/Shutterstock; 22 Cristi 180884/Shutterstock; 24 Vladimir Mucibabic/Shutterstock; 26 The Protected Art Archive/Alamy; 28l Robyn Mackenzie/Shutterstock, r Hintau Aliaksei/Shutterstock; 29t Paris Pierce/Alamy, b Dattatreya/Alamy
Front cover: Vladimir Mucibabic/Shutterstock

DAD0049
3-2011

9 8 7 6 5 4 3 2 1

3 4050 00098 9884

Contents

Perfect Prop Magic

IF YOU WANT to become a magician, then you need plenty of props—in other words, objects to help you perform tricks. Props are a fantastic way of making a magic act colorful, varied, and fun for the audience. Choose your props well and handle them skillfully, and you can create a memorable act.

PARTY TRICKS

Most prop tricks are too small to be seen from a large stage in a theater, so they are ideal for performing at a party or on a small stage. This kind of magic is traditionally called **parlor magic** because it was shown in a parlor, which was a room where people entertained guests. Nowadays, it is often called **cabaret magic**.

The great thing about parlor magic is that you are close to your audience, so you can chat with them and involve them in tricks.

SPECIAL STUFF

You can buy all kinds of magic props—for example, containers with secret compartments, double-sided cards, or extra-fine thread for suspending objects in the air. Some stage magicians use even bigger props, such as tables that **levitate** using hidden wires or supports.

PRACTICAL PROPS

The good news is that you don't have to buy a lot of expensive gadgets to do great prop magic. Many tricks use simple items such as scarves or rope. You can also perform amazing magic with ordinary objects such as balloons, drinking straws, and paper. This book will give you lots of ideas.

TRICK OF THE TRADE
Don't use too many specially-made props in your act. Do plenty of tricks with ordinary objects—they are more impressive, especially if people can look at the props afterward and check they're real!

Tricks in which assistants appear to be cut in half need large props and work best on a stage.

MASTER MAGICIAN

JEAN EUGENE ROBERT-HOUDIN (1805–1871)

The French magician Jean Eugene Robert-Houdin was a brilliant prop inventor. He trained as a watchmaker but learned magic tricks in his spare time. He was especially fascinated by moving mechanical figures, called **automata**, and began making his own to use in tricks. Soon he became a full-time magician, amazing audiences in small theaters around Europe with his wonderful props, each more imaginative than the last. One famous automaton was a miniature orange tree that appeared to grow flowers and then real oranges. One of the oranges split open and two clockwork butterflies fluttered into the air, holding up a handkerchief borrowed from a volunteer!

This is one of Robert-Houdin's expertly crafted and amazingly detailed mechanical models.

Tricks of the Trade

GREAT PROP MAGIC relies on three Ps: practice, **patter**, and performance. Practice always comes first. Never show a trick until you have learned it perfectly. Memorize each step of the trick and learn to handle the props gracefully so your movements are smooth and slick. Remember, everyone will be watching your hands, so you can't afford to be clumsy!

TRICK OF THE TRADE
Practice prop tricks in front of a mirror, or even better, film yourself. It will help you see whether you look comfortable with your props and whether you're holding them properly.

PERFECT PATTER

Once you've practiced a trick, plan what to say when you perform it. This is your patter. Patter helps you introduce and explain tricks and keeps your audience entertained. It is also a great way of **misdirecting** attention when there are things you don't want people to notice.

GO FOR IT!

Famous magicians aren't successful just because of their magic skills—they are great entertainers too. This is why you need to grab your audience's attention and keep it through the show. Be enthusiastic about your tricks, show props with style, and above all, be confident. You can find performance tips on page 28–29.

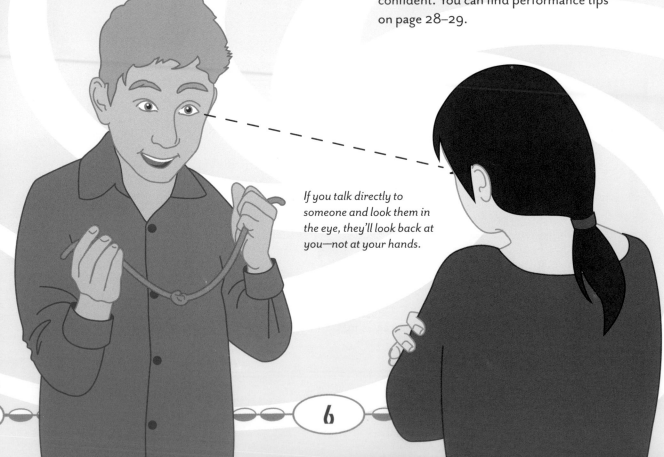

If you talk directly to someone and look them in the eye, they'll look back at you—not at your hands.

THE TORN PAPER CHALLENGE

Here's a trick to get you started. Practice until you can do it smoothly,
work out some patter that misdirects attention, and then perform it with confidence.

1. First, tell the audience you need a prop from the bathroom. Find a roll of toilet paper. Before you return, tear off a piece, scrunch it into a tiny wad, and wedge it behind your right ear.

wad of paper

2. Say that this is a trick you can all do. Hand a piece of toilet paper to each person and take one yourself. Ask everyone to tear up their piece and squish it into a ball.

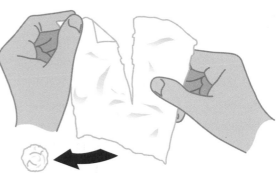

Pretend it's important for everyone to copy you exactly. They will be so focused on their piece that they won't see the one behind your ear!

3. Tell everyone to knead the ball with an elbow. Say that if they do this well enough, the bits will incredibly join up again. As you do this, secretly move the hidden wad of paper into your right hand.

4. Try kneading the ball with your fingers, too. Bring your hands together to show how. As you do, secretly swap the wads so the torn bits are in your right hand.

5. Go back to kneading with your elbow, and secretly drop the torn wad down the back of your shirt. Say that you think the paper is just about ready.

No one will notice your sneaky moves when they're busy with their own paper.

6. Slowly and carefully unfold your paper. It's whole again . . . unlike everyone else's!

MASTER MAGICIAN

JOHNNY THOMPSON (born 1934)

The American magician Johnny Thompson performed a comedy parlor magic act for many years. Calling himself "The Great Tomsoni," he pretended to be a pompous, silly magician who never had much luck with props. For example, he produced doves from a silk handkerchief and made sure they pooped on his suit to amuse the audience!

Magic Wands

A WAND IS a classic magic prop. It can be part of a trick, but it is also a great help in misdirecting attention. For example, a magician may reach into a pocket for a wand while secretly grabbing something else too, or distract you by waving it in the air. You can buy plastic or wooden wands and wands with hidden **gimmicks**, such as fake flowers that spring from the end.

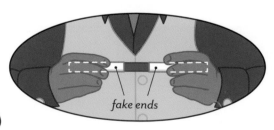

This wand is attached to a glove, so you can make it appear to levitate!

Making a Wand

It's easy to make your own wand using thick black paper rolled into a thin tube with a strip of white paper around each end.

Remember, no one will be handling the wand or getting close to it, so it doesn't matter if it's made of paper! Once you have your wand, try these quick tricks with it.

The Shrinking Wand

You can do this with a wand you've made yourself. You need two extra strips of white paper.

1. Roll the extra strips around the ends of the wand and stick them down. Make sure they are a little loose, so they slide along the wand.

2. Now you're ready. Hold the wand at the ends, like this. Tell the audience you can make your wand smaller so it fits in your pocket.

3. Slowly move your hands together so the fake ends slide along and the real ends of the wand are hidden in your hands.

TRICK OF THE TRADE
Put your wand away as soon as you finish, so no one sees the false ends. Slide them off the wand before you bring it out again.

original strip

extra strip

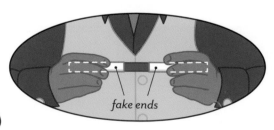

fake ends

4. To finish the trick, reverse the movement so the wand seems to grow again.

MAGNETIC MOVING WAND

This trick relies on excellent misdirection skills. Keep everyone's attention fixed on your hand and the wand rather than your face!

1. Tell the audience that you can make your wand magnetic. Make a big deal of placing it on a table and making stroking movements with your hand around it.

The more complicated you make these movements, the closer the audience will watch.

2. Say that the wand should now be magnetized and will follow your hand. Move your hand away from you and the wand. As you do this, gently blow on the wand to make it roll.

Practice blowing without moving your mouth much. You only need one long, slow puff.

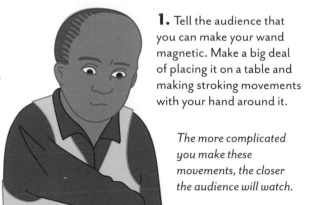

IMPOSSIBLE PURSE

Here's a funny way of producing a wand. You'll need an old purse to cut up.

1. Beforehand, take a small purse and make a hole in a bottom corner just big enough for your wand to slip through. Hide your wand down your sleeve with the end poking into the purse.

2. Come on stage holding the purse casually. Tell people you keep your wand in it. Unzip it and pretend to rummage around for the wand, and then slowly pull it up through the purse!

audience's view

Practice holding the purse in a natural way.

Silks, Scarves, and Hankies

ANOTHER CLASSIC MAGIC prop is a large silk handkerchief or scarf, often called a silk. Magicians use silks in many vanishing or appearing tricks and often knot them together to make a colorful rope. You can buy silks from magic shops, cut squares of thin material, or just use big hankies or napkins.

KNOTTY PROBLEMS

Try these puzzles on your friends to get used to handling silks.

1. First, lay a silk on the table. Invite a volunteer to hold the ends and tie a knot without letting go of either end.

2. When they give up, show them the secret: cross your arms before you take hold of the ends . . .

3. . . . and unfold your arms to transfer the knot to the silk!

4. Next, ask the volunteer to tie two silks together—for example, red and blue. Now ask them to tie a third one between the red and blue silks without untying them.

5. When they give up again, show them the answer: tie the third silk to the free ends of the others!

TRICK OF THE TRADE
Adapt the Impossible Purse trick on page 9 to introduce silks. Tie several silks together, hide them up your sleeve, and slowly pull them out from an impossibly small container!

HOLEY HANKY

With a little practice, you can appear to push a pencil right though a silk without making a hole.

1. Make a circle with the fingers and thumb of your left hand.

2. Drape a silk over the hand. Now make a dip in the middle of the silk with the first finger of your right hand.

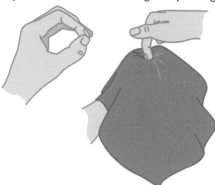

3. As you push in your finger, part your left fingers and thumb. Now drag the second finger of your right hand across, as if to widen the dip. In fact, you pull the material with you and create a gap in the silk.

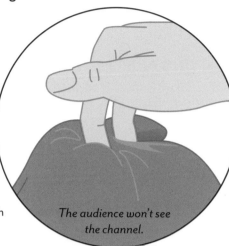

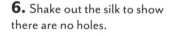

The audience won't see the channel.

4. Pick up a pencil with your right hand and push it into the gap. It looks as if it's going into the silk. Pretend to make an effort to push it through.

5. Let it go through the gap and pull it out from underneath. It looks as though it went through the silk!

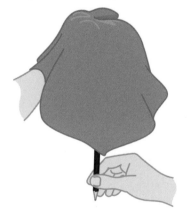

6. Shake out the silk to show there are no holes.

A good follow-up trick is Magic Fountain on page 13.

MASTER MAGICIAN

BILLY McCOMB (1922–2006)

Billy McComb was a skilled parlor magician who came from Northern Ireland. He performed around the United Kingdom and later in Hollywood. He also wrote magic books and worked as an adviser to other magicians, helping them with tricky **routines**.

Billy created many effects with silks. In one trick, silks appeared to change color, and then became half one color and half a different color. In another trick, he strolled around the audience, producing silks as he went, and then pulled a live chicken out of the bundle he had collected.

Brilliant Balloons

BALLOONS ARE FANTASTIC magic props. They're cheap to buy, colorful to look at, and loud when they burst—perfect for grabbing attention! Here are some ways to use balloons in your magic act.

TRICK OF THE TRADE
Use good-quality balloons because they are thicker and less likely to burst at the wrong moment.

Unburstable Balloons

The simplest trick you can do with a balloon is to secretly put a piece of clear tape on it, and then take a long pin and carefully poke it into the balloon through the tape. It doesn't burst!

Now try this: you pop a balloon and not only does it stay up, but it changes color too!

1. Before the trick, put one balloon inside another. Make sure they're different colors.

2. Blow up the balloons and tie each one. You'll need to blow into the outer balloon a little before you can get the inner one started.

3. When you perform the trick, say, "I wish this balloon were yellow. Hang on a minute . . ." Take the audience by surprise by popping the outer balloon with a pin, revealing the second balloon inside. Say, "That's better!"

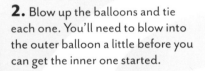

MASTER MAGICIAN

JEFF McBRIDE (born 1959)

Jeff McBride is an inventive U.S. magician who mixes small **sleight-of-hand** tricks with elaborate **illusions**. He has invented all kinds of prop tricks, including the water-spraying balloon effect on page 13. He used it to make water appear from all kinds of things, including a wad of toilet paper and a newspaper. Maybe you can invent your own water fountain trick!

MAGIC FOUNTAIN

Your audience won't suspect a balloon is involved in this trick if you perform it as part of a general prop routine without a balloon in sight.

1. Beforehand, pour a little water into a balloon. You don't need much—the balloon shouldn't be stretched.

2. Tie a knot in the neck of the balloon. It should be limp enough to hide in your hand.

3. Lay the balloon on a cutting board, take a pin, and carefully push about eight holes through the balloon. Because the balloon is so floppy, the water won't leak out.

4. Hide the balloon up your sleeve. Now you're ready to perform. Shake out a hanky or silk, and show the audience that it's empty.

5. Put the silk in your hand and fluff it up. As you do this, secretly pull the balloon from your sleeve and hide it in the middle of the silk.

6. Say that the secret of the trick is invisible water. Take an empty jug and pretend to pour the contents into the silk. Now pretend there's an invisible fountain spraying out. Of course no one will be impressed!

balloon hidden up sleeve

7. Say, "Oh, were you expecting real water? OK . . ." Wave your hand over the silk, gently squeeze the balloon, and water will squirt everywhere! Then stuff the silk and balloon into your pocket.

Make sure you're not too far from the audience. It's more fun if you spray them with water!

Paper Props

PROPS MADE FROM paper can be surprisingly effective as part of a magic act. You can use strips of newspaper, ordinary white or colored paper, or buy shiny wrapping paper if you want something that looks special. Try these paper loop tricks and impress your friends!

ONE-SIDED PAPER

This simple effect relies on one vital move—a sneaky twist of your paper strip as you make it into a loop.

1. Cut a strip of paper about three feet (1 m) long (you may need to tape a few shorter strips together) and hold it out. Tell the audience it's a magic strip of paper because it only has one side. Ask a volunteer to help you prove it.

2. Make the strip into a loop. As you do this, twist one of the ends over. Tape the ends together.

3. Ask your volunteer to take a thick pen and draw a line all along one side of the paper until they get back to where they began.

Practice making this twist with a casual turn of your wrist, so no one notices. Misdirect people's attention as you do it by talking or asking the volunteer to fetch some tape.

4. The line will go on . . . and on . . . and the volunteer will eventually realize they've covered both sides of the paper. Say, "See? I told you this paper only had one side!"

Going Loopy

This is a very old, famous trick that is often called the Afghan Bands. You need to practice your paper twisting so no one notices that each loop is slightly different.

1. Prepare three long strips of paper, each about 1 inch (2.5 cm) wide and 5 feet (1.5 m) long.

2. Show all three strips to the audience. Then take the first one and tape it into a big loop. Make a snip in the middle of the strip with a pair of scissors, and then carefully cut all the way around the loop.

3. When you've finished, you'll have two thin loops. Now ask a volunteer to copy what you did.

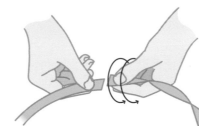

4. While the volunteer is coming up, take the second strip and make it into a loop. This time, sneakily twist one end of the strip, like you did in the One-Sided Paper trick.

5. As the volunteer cuts their strip, it becomes one enormous, thin loop. Pretend to be surprised.

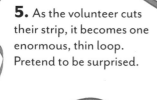

6. Ask a different volunteer to try. This time, twist the strip around twice, so the loop has two twists in it. Remind them that they should copy you and produce two loops.

7. When they've finished, your volunteer will find that they have two loops joined together!

How did that happen?

MASTER MAGICIAN

Jade

Jade was born in Indonesia, grew up in Taiwan, and now lives in the United States. She became successful with her elegant stage illusions and now tours worldwide. Jade makes her act memorable by using many beautiful props made out of paper, such as parasols and flowers. In one of her best-known illusions, she creates butterflies from paper, which gracefully flutter into the air above the stage.

Cool Tube Tricks

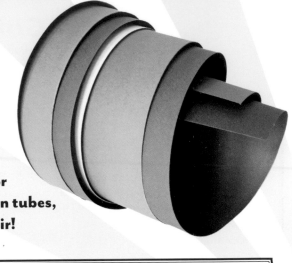

IF YOU'RE FEELING creative, why not use some paper or tagboard to make yourself a magic tube or two? These rolls, which are often called production tubes, are great for making silks appear as if out of thin air!

THE MAGIC TUBE

To make this tube, you will need two identical pieces of thick paper or card stock, scissors, tape, and a silk.

1. Roll one piece of paper into a fat cone shape. Make sure that the narrow end of the cone is only slightly smaller than the other end. Tape it in place.

2. Roll the second piece of paper around the cone to make a tube shape, and tape it in place. Make sure both ends are the same width as the wide end of the cone. Decorate the outer tube if you want.

3. Carefully stuff your silk into the gap between the narrow end of the cone and the outer tube. Now you're ready to perform.

4. Tell the audience you have a magic tube. Show them your tube face on, holding it at the end where the material is hidden. Let someone look into it briefly to confirm there's nothing in it.

5. Say, "Are you sure about that?" and whip out the silk!

Tube in a Tube

**Here's a trick with three tubes,
although the audience only sees two of them.**

1. Take three sheets of black card stock. Trim one sheet so it's an inch (2.5 cm) smaller than the first. Then trim the third to be smaller still.

window

2. Roll the sheets into tubes and tape them in place. Cut a long window in the biggest tube, and then paint or decorate the biggest and middle-sized tubes.

3. Slide the middle tube inside the big tube. Stuff silks or hankies tightly inside the small tube and put it in the middle one. Now you're ready to perform.

4. Tell the audience you have two tubes. Lift up the big tube, show people it's empty, and then replace it.

5. Next take out the second, middle tube and show that it's empty. The big tube now appears to be empty, too. Replace the middle tube.

6. Snap your fingers or say magic words, then reach into the small tube, and dramatically pull out the silks.

MASTER MAGICIAN

JOHN NEVIL MASKELYNE
(1839–1917)

John Nevil Maskelyne was an English magician who first trained as a watchmaker, so he was skilled at putting together intricate, complicated machinery. He created many clever props to use in his illusions. His most famous invention involves pushing a coin into a slot, which then makes a device click shut. Can you guess what it is? Find the answer on page 32.

TRICK OF THE TRADE
Try using handfuls of ribbons or party streamers for the Tube in a Tube trick. They will be effective when you pull them out and scatter them everywhere!

Matchbox Magic

ORDINARY MATCHBOXES CAN be turned into props for tricks in front of a small audience. Just remember that matches are dangerous! Ask an adult to remove any unused matches, and only use empty boxes in your tricks.

STOP THE BOX!

Use a big matchbox for this trick, so your audience can see it better. Make the box look more exciting by decorating it with shiny paper or stickers. This will also help to misdirect the audience's attention from your hands.

1. Make a hole with a pin at each end of the matchbox tray. Widen the holes using a pencil.

2. Trim a used match with scissors and wedge it across the inside of the tray.

3. Now thread a long piece of string through the holes and over the match. The string should slide through easily.

4. Put the sleeve back on the box. Now you're ready to perform. Hold the string loosely at each end and tip it from side to side. Say that you can magically control this box. In fact, you can make it defy gravity!

5. Hold the string vertically, with the box in your hand at the top. Now let go so the box slides down the string. When it gets near the middle, shout, "STOP!" At the same time, pull the string tight. The box will stop.

STOP!

string pulled tight

6. Wait a few moments, then shout, "GO!" At the same time, relax the string —and the box will continue to slide.

Make your hand movements as small as you can, so people don't notice them.

THE MELTING MATCHBOX

The key to this trick is to use the smallest matchboxes you can find because you need to hide one in your hand.

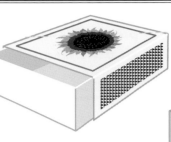

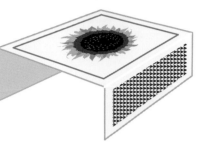

1. Find two identical matchboxes. Cut the bottom panel off one sleeve.

2. Lay a long piece of ribbon along the uncut matchbox sleeve, and then fit the cut sleeve on top. Now you're ready to perform.

3. Hold the matchbox upside down for the audience to see, and pull the ribbon a little to show that you've threaded one long piece through the sleeve.

Don't let anyone come too close!

4. Now push the tray into the sleeve and turn over the box. Say that you can use your body heat to melt the box off the ribbon.

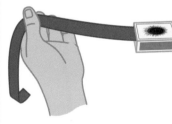

TRICK OF THE TRADE
Try strengthening the cut sleeve by unbending two paper clips, reshaping them to fit inside the sleeve, and then taping them inside. This will help the cut sleeve keep its shape and fit snugly over the real box.

5. Put down the box and rub your hands as you pretend to generate heat.

Then cup the box in both hands and secretly grip the cut sleeve in your palm.

6. Suddenly shake or bang the box on the table and whip your hands away. While everyone is looking at the separate ribbon and box, quickly drop the cut sleeve into your lap.

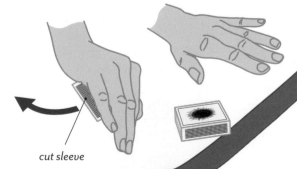

cut sleeve

Super Straws

A DRINKING STRAW is another prop that is easy to find and effective for magic tricks. Here are a few tricks with plastic straws that you can work into your act or use to impress your friends during lunch!

Clever Straw Lift

Here's a quick straw riddle to get you started. Challenge a friend to lift an empty bottle with a straw. When they give up, take the straw and bend it about two-thirds of the way down. Push the bent part into the bottle. The end will wedge itself against the side, letting you lift the bottle holding the top of the straw.

STRAW THROUGH A STRAW

This trick is straightforward—you just need to memorize the moves.

1. Take two plastic straws and let people examine them. Now hold them up in a cross shape, like this.

A   B

This is the magician's view.

2. Keep the straws pinched together with your left thumb and first finger. Wrap the bottom half of straw A up and around straw B, so it points downward again.

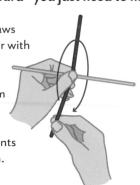

3. Swap your hands so you're keeping the straws in place with your right hand. Take the left half of straw B and wrap it around the top half of straw A.

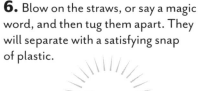

4. Next, wrap over that same half of straw B so it's facing to the right.

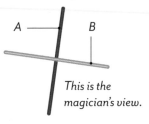

5. Now hold both ends of straw A in your left hand and both ends of straw B in your right hand. Tell the audience that you can separate the wrapped straws by forcing them through each other.

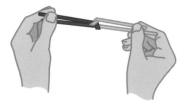

Don't pull the straws yet.

6. Blow on the straws, or say a magic word, and then tug them apart. They will separate with a satisfying snap of plastic.

CUT . . . AND UNCUT

In this ingenious trick, you appear to cut a piece of string and then join the ends again.

1. Before the trick, cut a slit about 2 inches (6 cm) long in the middle of a plastic straw. Do this by pricking a hole with a pin and then carefully snipping along with small scissors.

2. When you perform the trick, hold the straw with the slit facing you. Thread string through the straw.

3. Fold the straw in half. As you do this, pull down on both ends of the string so that it comes out through the slit. Make sure your fingers cover this bit of string.

This is what the audience doesn't see.

4. Take a large pair of scissors and cut through the folded middle of the straw.

5. Make sure everyone can see the two cut halves of straw sticking up.

6. Now cover the cut ends with your hand. Say some magic words, or wave your other hand over the straw. Then slowly pull out the string. It's one long piece!

Don't let anybody study the two straw halves, or they may notice the slit.

TRICK OF THE TRADE
To make people assume your straw is ordinary, pull it from a whole pack of straws at the start of the trick. As long as you've removed all the other straws of the same color, you'll know which one to pick!

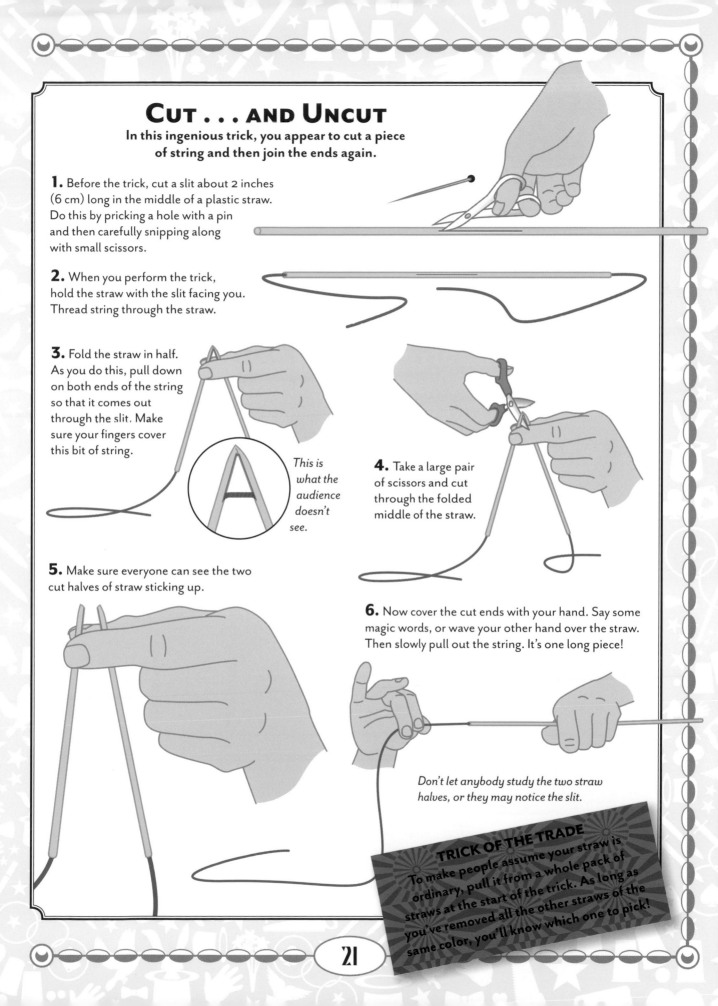

Rope Magic

ROPE IS A classic magic prop in all kinds of tricks. You can cut it, knot it, or even make things appear to move through it. Magicians use a soft, thick cord for rope tricks. You can buy your own from magic shops—or just find a length of cotton clothesline.

THE ONE-HANDED INSTANT KNOT

Here's a neat way of tying a knot in a piece of rope using just a shake of your hand! Practice until you can do steps 2 and 3 really quickly.

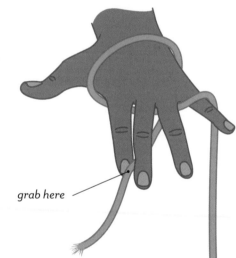

grab here

1. Hold up a length of rope, and then lay it over your hand, like this.

make sure this end is shorter

2. Tilt your hand downward and trap the shorter end between your first and second fingers.

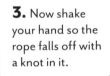

3. Now shake your hand so the rope falls off with a knot in it.

TENKAI (1889–1972)

Tenkai was a Japanese magician who created many famous sleight-of-hand effects with props such as playing cards, coins, and rope. In one trick, he appeared to pull a knotted rope through his neck. In fact, the rope was cleverly looped, creating the illusion of a knot. He is honored in Japan with the annual Tenkai Prize, which is awarded to inventors of great magical effects.

THE CUT AND MENDED ROPE

This is a version of a famous rope trick in which a rope is cut and then magically joined again.

1. Hold up a length of rope, and then grasp it in your left hand.

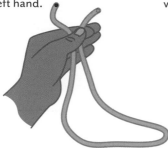

2. Grip the end of the loop with your right index and middle fingers with your thumb inside the loop.

3. Lift the loop up to your left hand and use your right thumb and index finger to grab the end on the right.

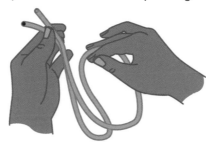

4. Now pull up some rope to form a loop, which you hold in place with your left thumb. It should look as if you are holding the original loop in your hand. In fact, you've created a fake loop.

Practice until you can do steps 3 and 4 quickly.

5. Ask a volunteer to cut the loop.

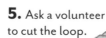

6. Let the ends on the far left and right fall down, so you seem to be holding two cut pieces of rope.

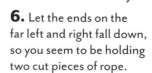

7. Say that you know an amazing way of joining the ends again. Tie a single knot in the two cut ends.

8. Display the "mended" rope. Appear offended that no one's impressed! In fact, the knot is a on a separate short bit of rope.

Keep the knot hidden in your right fist—drop it out of sight while people admire the magically mended rope.

9. Say you'll try again. Bunch up the rope in your fists and blow on it, or say magic words. Then slide your hands off the rope, secretly sliding off the fake knot, too.

TRICK OF THE TRADE
Another way of getting rid of the knot is to cut it off, leaving you without a bit of rope to hide.

Hoops and Rings

HOOPS MAKE VERY useful props. Although you can buy special hoops that link and unlink, there are plenty of tricks that use ordinary bangles and rings. Here are some great ideas to get you started.

TRAP THE BANGLE!

The secret of this trick is to have two identical bangles. You also need to wear a jacket with an inside pocket.

1. Before the trick, hide one bangle up your sleeve. Hold the other in your hand.

hidden identical bangle

2. Ask a volunteer to tie the ends of a piece of rope around your wrists. Tell them to be sure you can't pull your hands free.

3. Now say that you will magically trap the bangle on the rope in the time it takes you to turn around. As you turn, slip the bangle into your inside pocket, and pull out the hidden bangle.

Slip the bangle into an inside pocket . . .

. . . as you pull out the hidden bangle from your sleeve.

4. When you face the audience again, it looks as if the bangle has jumped on to the rope.

CHING LING FOO (1854–1922)

Ching Ling Foo was an amazing Chinese magician. His acts included illusions such as breathing clouds of smoke and plumes of fire. He was also one of the first performers of the Chinese Linking Rings trick, in which large metal hoops appear to link and unlink. Many magicians copied his tricks in their own acts, including one man who gave himself the similar-sounding stage name of Chung Ling Soo even though he wasn't Chinese. You can read more about Chung Ling Soo (and his fatal prop mistake) on page 29.

Ching Ling Foo.

THE ESCAPING RING

In this trick, you perform a sleight-of-hand move right in front of the audience. Practice it well, be confident, and use lots of patter to misdirect attention.

1. Borrow someone's ring and thread it on to a long piece of rope. Display it in your left hand, like this.

2. With your right hand, hold the rope just below your left hand. At the same time, close your left hand around the ring and turn it downward. As you do this, secretly let the ring drop down into your right hand.

This is the view from your side.

3. Right away, wrap the rope in your right hand over your left hand and pull it out away from you, all the time slipping the ring along inside your right fist until the ring comes off the end and into your fist. Ask a volunteer to hold the end of the rope.

4. Take the other end in your right hand and bring it across over your left hand. Ask another volunteer to hold this end.

second volunteer

ring still hidden in right fist

5. Say that there's no way you can get the ring off the rope. Or is there? Hold your right fist (with the ring still in it) under your left one. Rub them together or shake them. Then open your right hand to reveal the ring!

ring hidden in right fist

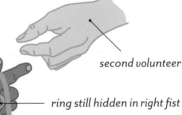

first volunteer

Great Escapes

IF YOU CAN free rings from a piece of rope, why not try freeing yourself? This type of magic is called **escapology**, and it involves escaping from traps such as ropes, handcuffs, cages, or boxes—or all of them at once! Escapologists often put themselves in real danger, but you should never try anything risky yourself—leave that to the experts.

DANGEROUS DEEDS

Some escapology routines use trick techniques such as fake knots, while others rely on the magician knowing how to pick locks or wriggle free of **restraints**. Here's an example of a simple escape.

1. The magician climbs into a sack and secretly pulls down a loop of rope. An assistant ties the sack tightly.

2. Hidden behind a screen, the magician opens the top of the sack wide enough to reach up and untie the knot.

MASTER MAGICIAN

HARRY HOUDINI
(1874–1926)

EUROPE'S ECLIPSING SENSATION
HOUDINI
THE WORLD'S HANDCUFF KING & PRISON BREAKER

NOTHING ON EARTH CAN HOLD HOUDINI A PRISONER

The most famous escapologist of all time is the Hungarian-born magician Harry Houdini. His real name was Ehrich Weiss, but he called himself Houdini after the conjurer Robert-Houdin (see page 5). Houdini began his career as a card magician but soon started doing escape acts. As his fame grew, his escapes became more and more daring and difficult. He freed himself from padlocked chests, nailed-down crates, and prison cells. He got out of straitjackets while hanging upside down from his ankles and from a glass tank filled with water. For this last escape, he had to hold his breath for more than three minutes!

THE HANDS-TIED TABLE LEG ESCAPE

This easy escapology trick will baffle your friends.

1. Ask a volunteer to tie the ends of a piece of rope around your wrists to form a pair of handcuffs. Tell them to make as many knots as they like and make sure you can't slip the loop over your hand.

The rope shouldn't be so tight that it hurts your wrists.

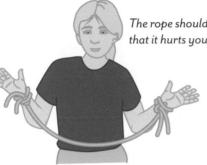

2. Now ask your volunteer to loop a second rope over the one tied to your wrists and to tie each end to a table leg.

3. Say that you will now attempt to free yourself from the table in just five seconds. Ask volunteers to put something heavy on the table, so you can't lift the legs. Now you need a volunteer or assistant to hide you from view, for example by moving a table or screen in front.

4. As the audience starts counting, move closer to the table and pull the second rope toward you.

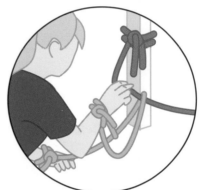

5. Feed the loop up through the rope around your left wrist. Don't twist it.

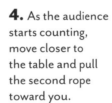

6. Pull the loop up and over your left hand.

7. Slip the loop under the rope around your wrist, and then pull it back over your hand. You should now be free!

view from the back

8. Spring out from behind your screen just before the time runs out.

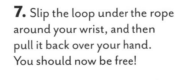

TRICK OF THE TRADE
Challenge people to copy your escape. Tie them up in the same way and watch them get in a tangle!

Show Time!

ONCE YOU'VE LEARNED some prop tricks and practiced until you can do them in your sleep, you're ready to stage your own magic show! Here are lots of helpful hints and tips to make sure your act is a big hit.

TRICK OF THE TRADE
If you perform a lot, paper and tagboard props will soon get worn or bent, so replace them regularly. Make sure ropes aren't frayed, and wash and iron silks.

Lee J. da Man

A PROP BOX

One essential item is a container for your props. Make sure it looks attractive or exciting—no one will be impressed if you come on stage with a plastic bag. Decorate a large cardboard box or search charity shops for an interesting old suitcase. Whatever you use, make sure it has a cover to stop people taking a close look at things you don't want them to see!

Pack your box so the things you need first are on top. It's also a good idea to carry spares of props that might break.

WHAT TO WEAR

Magicians wear all kinds of costumes. Some dress as clowns. Others try for a mysterious look with a suit or cloak. For parlor magic, choose something simple that doesn't take attention from your props. Also, remember that some tricks need long sleeves or handy pockets.

Brightly-patterned outfits can make it hard for the audience to see props clearly. The plainer your clothes, the more your props stand out.

MASTER MAGICIAN

CHUNG LING SOO (1861–1918)

Chung Ling Soo was the stage name of William Ellsworth Robinson, a magician who specialized in grand illusions with lots of props. In his most famous trick, a marked bullet was fired at him from a gun. He appeared to catch the bullet in his hand or mouth. When Soo performed the trick one night in 1918, the bullet hit him in the chest. He died the next day in the hospital. Can you figure out how he did the bullet trick and why it went wrong? See page 32 for the answer.

PERFORMANCE TIPS

Plan your act carefully to keep your audience entertained. Start with something exciting and include a variety of props—but don't go on for too long. If you're good at telling jokes, make your patter cheerful and funny. If you prefer to say less, play music, but don't perform in silence.

DISASTER!

Performing with props is nerve-wracking. What if something breaks or someone works out the secret behind a trick? If you handle your props confidently, you'll avoid a lot of problems. If something does go wrong, keep cool! Shrug it off or make a joke, and then go on to the next trick. As long as the audience is having fun, they won't mind.

Being a magician is like acting in a play. Create a character and throw yourself into the part!

Glossary

automaton (plural: automata)
a mechanical moving object, for example, a cuckoo in a cuckoo clock; There are many different types of automata, used as toys, tools, and magical props.

cabaret magic
a modern name for parlor magic; A cabaret is a show in a nightclub or restaurant.

escapology
a type of magic that involves escaping from restraints or dangerous situations; Some magicians mix escapology tricks with other types of magic to keep their audiences entertained.

gimmick
a secret part or object, for example, a false bottom or hidden spring that makes a trick work

illusion
an effect that tricks you into thinking something impossible is happening; Some magicians perform big, spectacular illusions on stage, for example, levitating or sawing a person in half.

levitate
to be suspended without any visible support, seeming to defy gravity

misdirecting
drawing an audience's attention away from something you don't want them to see or think too much about

parlor magic
a type of magic that is performed for small audiences, traditionally in someone's house rather than on a stage in a theater

patter
prepared, practiced speech that magicians use when performing magic tricks; Although you need to work out your patter beforehand, make sure you speak naturally and don't read it out like a script.

restraint
something that ties, fastens, or traps you in place, for example a rope, chains, or handcuffs

routine
a set or sequence of tricks

sleight-of-hand
the technique of secretly moving, altering, or swapping objects to create a magical effect; Sleights (pronounced "slights") take a lot of practice to perform well and rely on good misdirection skills.

Web Sites

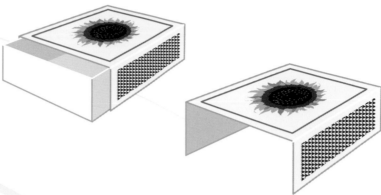

www.magictricks.com/library
Read biographies of famous magicians and discover fascinating facts about their lives and the tricks they invented.

www.activitytv.com/magic-tricks-for-kids
Find great tricks that use all kinds of props, including rope, silks, straws, and much more. You can search for tricks by skill level, or browse them all.

www.freemagictricks4u.com/free-best-magic-tricks.html
Watch a helpful video tutorial for the Melting Matchbox trick on page 19. Then click on the street magic link at the bottom of the page to find many more prop tricks.

www.magicsam.com/index.asp
Find out about The Society of American Magicians, the oldest magical society in the world, which was once headed by Harry Houdini. Read about recent magic news and find S. A. M. assemblies in your area!

www.magician.org/
Learn about the history of the International Brotherhood of Magicians, the world's largest organization for those interested in or practicing magic. Find magic shows, lectures, and conventions near you!

Index

SECRETS OF MAGIC . . . REVEALED!

Page 17: What did John Nevil Maskelyne invent?

Answer: He invented the first pay toilet! The door would only shut if a penny was put in the lock. His invention is still used around the world today.

Page 29: How could Chung Ling Soo catch a bullet?

Answer: The trick worked like this: the bullet was marked by a volunteer. Then Soo appeared to pass it to an assistant to load into the gun. In fact, he hid the bullet in his hand, and the assistant loaded a different one. The gun was real, but it was rigged so it made a bang and smoked but didn't fire a bullet. It was easy for Soo to hold up the marked bullet as if he had caught it out of the air. The night the trick went wrong, the gun really did fire the bullet that had been loaded into it, and it hit Soo.